Dear Carmen,
Thank you for your

Jazz, Java & Jesus

Support!
May the Lord bless and
Keep you and your family.

Warmly,
Aleyshd R. Proctor
2010

Jazz, Java & Jesus

Christian Devotions to
Soothe Your Soul

Aleysha R. Proctor

To order additional copies of this book, contact:
Xlibris Corporation
1-888-795-4274
www.Xlibris.com
Orders@Xlibris.com
43007

CONTENTS

FOREWORD

Jazz, Java & Jesus. Why Jazz? Jazz, because I love smooth jazz music. Many times, it's soothing jazz music that ushers me into worshipping the Lord over other kinds of music. In 1 Samuel 16, King Saul is distressed and troubled and one of his servants tells him that he needs David, the shepherd boy, to come and play his harp for him and then he'll be at peace. The Bible tells us that Saul would be "refreshed and well" after David played for him.

Why Java? Java, because I love coffee too! It's times when I'm having a cup of coffee (decaf, of course!) that I can relax and think of the goodness of the Lord. Even if I'm having coffee with friends, I'm usually meditating and talking to God. Jesus told the Samaritan woman in John 4 that true worshippers won't worship God at a certain time or place, but will worship Him in spirit and in truth (all the time) because He is a spirit and seeks to be worshipped all the time.

Why Jesus? WHO ELSE?! Because I love Jesus, because He's the Keeper of my soul, because He's my Savior, because He's the only true and living God, because He's my Healer, because He's my Friend, because He comforts me, because He prays for me, because He holds my future. Do I need to go on?

Jazz, Java & Jesus – the perfect combination to soothe the weary soul and to remind you that YOU are, indeed, important to the Lord!

God bless you.

All Things Beautiful!

He has made everything beautiful in its time.

—Ecclesiastes 3:11a

For the last few months, these three words, "All things beautiful," have kept coming up in my spirit. I realized that it was the Holy Spirit bringing back the Word of God to keep me encouraged and hopeful during the times when things looked like all things *except* beautiful.

As we recently welcomed in the New Year, you would have been hard pressed to find someone who didn't want to see 2008 make its exit. There was talk on the news channels, in the newspapers, on the radio, from the pulpit, and in general conversations of how 2008 was a very challenging year for many people.

Ecclesiastes 3:11a tells us that the Lord makes *everything beautiful*—in its time. Prior to the eleventh verse, the scriptures tell us that *everything has a season*! A season! Let's look at it.

> **1** To everything there is a season, a time for every purpose under heaven:
> **2** A time to be born,
> And a time to die;
> A time to plant,
> And a time to pluck what is planted;
> **3** A time to kill,
> And a time to heal;

A time to break down,
And a time to build up;
4 A time to weep,
And a time to laugh;
A time to mourn,
And a time to dance;
5 A time to cast away stones,
And a time to gather stones;
A time to embrace,
And a time to refrain from embracing;
6 A time to gain,
And a time to lose;
A time to keep,
And a time to throw away;
7 A time to tear,
And a time to sew;
A time to keep silence,
And a time to speak;
8 A time to love,
And a time to hate. (Ecclesiastes 3:1-8)

A time of war,
And a time of peace.

It's comforting to know that wintertime always doesn't last! And neither does the hot, humid, hazy summertime. If you've been going through some challenging times, don't think that this is just the way life goes! Declare that you're just going *through a season*! God created seasons in the beginning, in Genesis 1. He was telling us from the start that things won't always be like this! Think about that for a minute.

Your next season is coming—your *due season*! Your season of blessings and breakthrough! Your season of abundance and favor! Your season of opportunities and miracles! Your season of good health and healing!

Remember, to *everything*, there is a season! It doesn't matter how things look right now, God has promised that He'll make *all things beautiful* in the right season!

Notes

And in *That* Name!

Let it be known to you all, and to all the people of Israel, that by the name of Jesus Christ of Nazareth, whom you crucified, whom God raised from the dead, by Him this man stands here before you whole. 11 This is the "Stone which was rejected by you builders, which has become the Chief Cornerstone." 12 Nor is there salvation in any other, for there is no other name under heaven given among men by which we must be saved.

—Acts 4:10-12

In a previous devotion, we determined that a name reveals the identity, nature, character, and essence of a person, place, or thing. I recently read a devotion by a well-known pastor who said that we should base our prayer request on God's character. He went on to say that we should pray like we *know* God will answer us by saying something like, "I'm expecting You to answer this prayer because of who You are."

Jesus said in John 14:13-14, "And whatever you ask in My name, that I will do, that the Father may be glorified in the Son. 14 If you ask anything in My name, I will do *it*."

In *Jesus's name!* Jesus said to pray in His name, and the well-known pastor suggested that we should base our prayer request on His character. So what is His character? Well, it's wrapped up in His name!

When Isaiah prophesied about Jesus's birth, he said, "And His NAME shall be called Wonderful Counselor, Mighty God, Everlasting Father, the Prince of Peace" (Isa. 9:6).

Jesus has over one hundred names in the Bible! Here are just a few.

Advocate (1 John 2:1)
Author and Perfecter of our Faith (Heb. 12:2)
Beginning and End (Rev. 22:13)
Bread of God (John 6:33)
Bread of Life (John 6:35; 6:48)
Bridegroom (Matt. 9:15)
Creator (John 1:3)
Deliverer (Rom. 11:26)
Eternal Life (1 John 1:2; 5:20)
Faithful and True (Rev. 19:11)
Faithful Witness (Rev. 1:5)
Good Shepherd (John 10:11,14)
Great High Priest (Heb. 4:14)
Head of the Church (Eph. 1:22; 4:15; 5:23)
Heir of all things (Heb. 1:2)
Holy and True (Rev. 3:7)
Hope (1 Tim. 1:1)
Hope of Glory (Col. 1:27)
Horn of Salvation (Luke 1:69)
Immanuel (Matt. 1:23)
Judge of the living and the dead (Acts 10:42)
Keeper of our souls (1 Pet. 2:25)
King of kings (1 Tim. 6:15; Rev. 19:16)
Lamb of God (John 1:29)
Life (John 14:6; Col. 3:4)
Light of the World (John 8:12)
Lion of the Tribe of Judah (Rev. 5:5)
Living Water (John 4:10)
Lord of lords (Rev. 19:16)
Morning Star (Rev. 22:16)
Only Begotten Son of God (John 1:18; 1 John 4:9)

Our Great God and Savior (Titus 2:13)
Our Holiness (1 Cor. 1:30)
Our Protection (2 Thess. 3:3)
Our Redemption (1 Cor. 1:30)
Our Righteousness (1 Cor. 1:30)
Our Sacrificed Passover Lamb (1 Cor. 5:7)
Power of God (1 Cor. 1:24)
Resurrection and Life (John 11:25)
Righteous Branch (Jer. 23:5)
Rock (1 Cor. 10:4)
Ruler of God's Creation (Rev. 3:14)
Savior (Eph. 5:23; Titus 1:4; 3:6; 2 Pet. 2:20)
Son of the Most High God (Luke 1:32)
The One Mediator (1 Tim. 2:5)
The Stone the builders rejected (Acts 4:11)
The Truth (John 1:14; 14:6)
The Way (John 14:6)
The Word of God (Rev. 19:13)

I'll bet *whatever* you need is wrapped up in His character, which is His name!

Notes

But God Is Faithful!

For as the rain comes down, and the snow from heaven, and do not return there, but water the earth, and make it bring forth and bud, that it may give seed to the sower and bread to the eater, 11 So shall My word be that goes forth from My mouth; It shall not return to Me void, but it shall accomplish what I please, and it shall prosper in the thing for which I sent it.

—Isaiah 55:10-11

God is faithful! There's so much hope in those three little words. When everything around us is shaky and unreliable, it's good to know that the God of the universe is faithful. Well, what is He faithful to? you may ask. He's faithful to the Word that He's spoken. Words that concern you and me. Words about our future. Words about our peace. Words about our health and well-being.

God has made us so many promises in the Bible—all of which He keeps! But if we can just be honest with ourselves, sometimes during the waiting season, we may give up, lose faith, and become discouraged. But that doesn't change the fact that God's Word has already gone forth, and whatever He's said *will* come to pass! In Isaiah 55, God said, "WHATEVER goes out of My mouth, WILL BE ACCOMPLISHED, it's impossible for My Words to come back to me EMPTY!"

Let me show you a promise that God made early in the Bible that took some time to come to pass. In the early chapters of Genesis, whatever God spoke was created right away! When He said, "Let there be light," the

16

Holy Spirit created light right away. However, when He said that He had created man *and* woman, Eve hadn't been created yet! In Genesis 1:27, it says, "So God created man in His own image, in the image of God created He him; male and female created He THEM." The Bible even goes on to say in Genesis 1:28 (before Eve is created), "Then God blessed THEM and said to THEM, 'Be fruitful and multiply; fill the earth and subdue it; have dominion over the fish of the sea, over the birds of the air, and over every living thing that moves on the earth." I'm sure the animals were thinking, "Who is this 'THEM' that He keeps talking about? I only see Adam." Could it be that God had already considered Eve created?! Even before she was made and brought to Adam. Whether anyone else saw her or not, God had spoken about her, and she *was* coming!

In Genesis 1:27, it says that God created male *and* female, but we don't hear about Eve being created until the next chapter, Genesis 2:22, where it says, "And the rib, which the Lord God had taken from man, made He a woman, and brought her unto the man."

Just as the many promises that He's made to you and me in His Word, we may not see them yet in our physical lives, but since God has spoken them—and if we can believe it—then *they're coming*! What prayers have you given up on? Dust them off and start believing God for the manifestation of them again!

Remember, the fish, birds, and even Adam hadn't seen Eve yet, but God said that He had created "woman."

Notes

Forgive and Be Forgiven!

For I will forgive their iniquity, and their sin I will remember no more.

—Jeremiah 31:34b

A friend of mine recently said, "When I forgive someone, I also tell them, 'It NEVER happened.'" Now that's forgiveness! When the person who was offended says, "I forgive you, and as far as I'm concerned, the offense never happened!" that's the kind of forgiveness that the Lord extends to us and expects us to extend toward others. He said in Isaiah 43:25, "I, even I, am He who blots out your transgressions for My own sake; and I will NOT remember your sins."

I'm sure you've heard people say, "I may forgive, but I won't forget!" Well, that's the same as saying that you truly haven't forgiven because God expects us not to bring up the offenses again, to forgive the person, to make a conscious effort to forget what happened, and to move on.

We only hurt ourselves when we keep a running list of what people have done to us or haven't done but that we found offensive. It's that thing that we're holding on to that's holding us back! Jesus said over and over to forgive so that the Lord can forgive you of your sins.

There's nothing that a human being can do to you that should stand in the way of the Lord's hearing your prayers! Jesus said in Mark 11:25-26, "And whenever you stand praying, if you have anything against anyone, forgive him, that your Father in heaven may also forgive you your trespasses. 26

But if you do not forgive, neither will your Father in heaven forgive your trespasses."

Sometimes it is hard to forgive and forget what mean things people have done to us. But just think how hard it must be for the Lord to forgive us when we commit sins against Him—but He does—and He not only forgives, but He gives us His Word that He won't even remember them! When Jesus was hanging on the cross—after being beaten, His flesh torn to pieces, pierced in His side, falsely accused, spat upon, crowned with thorns, and having spikes driven through His hands and feet—He looked up to heaven and said, "Father, forgive them. For they don't know what they're doing" (Luke 23:34).

Do you think Jesus was thinking about which one of the Roman soldiers put the crown of thorns on His head, or which ones were gambling over His clothes? No! He had truly forgiven them! I can't imagine what would have happened if He decided to hold a grudge or kept playing the offensives over and over again in His mind.

Forgive and let go and move on!

Notes

God Is Able!

Now to Him who is able to do exceedingly abundantly above all that we ask or think, according to the power that works in us, 21 to Him be glory in the church by Christ Jesus to all generations, forever and ever. Amen.

—Ephesians 3:20-21

Can I just be honest with you? Over the last few months, if not several months, I've been feeling like my energy and strength have been zapped. Do you know what I'm talking about?

Have you ever felt like you've done all that you can do and nothing has changed for the better in your life? Have you ever felt like you've hit a brick wall? Maybe you haven't, but you probably know someone else who has.

Faith has to be tested. And without tests, there are no testimonies! In Hebrews 11, a.k.a. "the Hall of Faith," the whole chapter talks about great men and women of God in the Old Testament who did great things *by faith*. It then goes on to say in verse 39, "And all these, having obtained a good testimony through faith."

I recently had dinner with a friend who is a believer in Christ who said to me that because of things going on in his life and the lives of other believers his faith is being tried. If you haven't had your faith tried yet, keep on living.

It's times like these when we have to reach into our spirits and pull out the Word and promises of God to keep us going. I love Ephesians 3:20.

We can stop at the first three words—"Now to Him" and get our shout on! No matter what you're going through, look unto the Lord and say, "Now to You!" All the mess that may be going on around me, but let me focus on the *Him* that Ephesians 3:20 is talking about. But the scripture doesn't stop there, it goes on to say that He is *able*! And not only is He able, but He's also able to do *exceedingly*, and not just exceedingly, but also *abundantly*, and not just exceedingly *and* abundantly, but also *above*! Above what? Above *all* (not some things, but *all* things) that we ask—and not just what we can ask for, but *also* He's able to do *exceedingly, abundantly, above all that we ask or think*! Ask or think?!

If things aren't working in our favor, maybe we've stopped asking God for blessings, or maybe we've stopped thinking about the promises of God. Maybe we've allowed the cares of the world to creep in and silence us from communicating with the only One who's able to do exceedingly, abundantly, above all that we ask or think! Keep reminding yourself that God *is* able!

Now to Him!

Notes

God Has a Plan. He Always Does!

"For I know the plans I have for you," declares the LORD, "plans to prosper you and not to harm you, plans to give you hope and a future."

—Jeremiah 29:11 (New International Version)

Isn't it refreshing to know that the Lord has plans for our lives? That we don't have to go through life solely based on the plans that we've created for ourselves? If we can just be honest about it, sometimes we don't have the best plans in mind. Sometimes our plans don't go as we hope they will, and sometimes, we just plainly and simply don't have any plans at all!

But the God of the universe has already mapped our lives out, and guess what, His plans are always glorious. And even if it takes us a while or a lifetime to reach the destiny that He's mapped out for us, *we will get there*!

Let's look at King David for a minute. While David was a young shepherd boy, Samuel, the man of God, comes to his house to find the next king that God had provided for Himself. In

1 Samuel 16:1, it says, "Now the LORD said to Samuel, 'How long will you mourn for Saul, seeing I have rejected him from reigning over Israel? Fill your horn with oil, and go; I am sending you to Jesse the Bethlehemite. For I have provided Myself a king among his sons.'"

Although David had been anointed as king as a young boy, he found himself in some troubled situations. He serves then King Saul faithfully, but King

Saul becomes jealous of him and tries to kill him. Imagine running for your life from the king and his men, hiding in caves, afraid to come out and face the world, yet *knowing* that God has anointed you! The Bible tells us that David had to encourage himself in the Lord.

To every plan, there is a process. And although God's Word came to David at an early age, it wasn't until he had been tested and pruned that the manifestation showed up. God always gets His way! Rest assured, if He's promised you something, then it *is* coming to pass! His Word says that He has *plans* to prosper you, and not to harm you, *plans* to give you a hope and a future!

He has *great plans* for *you*!

Notes

God Has Been Good *and* He's Been Better Than That!

And Israel said to Joseph, "I had not thought to see your face; but in fact, God has also shown me your offspring!"

—Genesis 48:11

If there's anything that I know for sure, it's that God is good all the time!

In the book of Genesis, God has told Abraham that He was going to make him the father of many nations. In chapter 17:19, God said that He was going to establish His covenant with Abraham's son, Isaac, who hasn't been born yet. In fact, God said I'm going to establish my covenant with Isaac and with his descendants after him. From Isaac comes Jacob, and from Jacob (God later changes his name to Israel) comes the twelve tribes of Israel. He had twelve sons, of which one was his favorite—Joseph.

Joseph was Jacob's favorite son, and his brothers knew it and hated him for it. In Genesis 37, his brothers have sold Joseph into slavery, but they tell their father that he was devoured by a wild beast. Needless to say, Jacob was devastated. In verses 34 and 35, he mourns for many days and refuses to be comforted. He even says, and I paraphrased, "Just let me die so I can be with Joseph."

Now to Jacob, who thinks that Joseph is dead and who's now too old to have any more children, there can't be twelve tribes of Israel, but only eleven.

While a severe famine has hit the land, Joseph is now prospering as governor of Egypt. His brothers have to travel to Egypt and ask to buy grain from him in order to survive. While his brothers, who sold him into slavery don't recognize him, Joseph inquires about the well-being of his father. He later reveals himself as Joseph, their brother, and tells them to tell their father that he's still alive.

The Bible tells us in Genesis 45:26 that Jacob's heart stood still at the news that Joseph was still alive! He then said in verse 28, "It is enough. Joseph, my son, is still alive. I will go and see him before I die." In other words, "God has been good!"

To our spiritual forefathers, large families and many generations were very important to them. And it's also important to God because God would always include a person's descendents in their blessings. Now, everyone has packed up to go to Egypt, including Jacob and his whole family. The Bible even names all his sons and their sons in chapter 46 verses 8 through 26. When Jacob sees Joseph, the Bible says that they hug and cry for a good while, then in verse 30, Jacob says, "Now let me die, since I have seen your face, because you are still alive." Again, God has been good!

Jacob is now 147 years old and getting ready to die. Joseph brings his sons to meet their grandfather for the first time. In chapter 48:8, Jacob says, "Who are these?" When Joseph introduces them as his sons, Jacob says in verse 11, "I had not thought to see your face; but in fact, God has also shown me your offspring!" In other words, "God's been better than good to me!"

After years of heartbreak and mourning over Joseph, the Lord blesses him before he closes his eyes to death to see Joseph again and his family members of the tribe of Joseph.

God has not stopped being good! Psalm 23 says, "SURELY goodness and mercy shall follow me ALL THE DAYS OF MY LIFE!" God has been good to each and every one of us, and He's been better than that.

No matter what you're going through, praise Him for His goodness toward you. As Dr. Marvin Sapp says in one of his songs, "Praise will confuse the enemy!" (See 2 Chronicles 20:22) If you want to get the devil off your back, praise God when you're going through tough times!

Psalm 107 says over and over, "Oh, that men would give thanks to the LORD for His goodness, and for His wonderful works to the children of men!"

Indeed, God has been good to us, and He's been better than that!

Notes

Goodness *and* Mercy!

Surely goodness and mercy shall follow me all the days of my life!

—Psalm 23:6a

I once heard a pastor say that God's goodness will give you the blessings that you don't deserve, and His mercy will keep off you the punishment that you do deserve!

God's goodness is described as His bounty (prosperity, provisions, and richness) to whomever He chooses to show His goodness. In many scripture passages, we see God's goodness *and* His mercy showing up at the same time.

In 2 Samuel 11, King David has taken another man's wife (Bathsheba), and she conceives a child by him while her husband is away on the battlefield. David then brings her husband home and tries to get him to go home and spend some time with his wife. When Uriah, her husband, doesn't do as David hopes he will, he then has him placed on the frontline of the hottest battle to make certain that Bathsheba becomes a widow, and then he can have her as his own wife.

When the prophet Nathan spoke to David about his sins in 2 Samuel 12, he spoke in a parable about a rich man with many flocks taking a poor man's one little lamb for his own. King David becomes angry and says whoever has done this will surely die! And Nathan says, "King David, you are that man!" He then points out how God has been *good* to him by saying in verse 7-8, "Thus says the LORD God of Israel: 'I anointed you king over Israel, and I delivered you from the hand of Saul. 8 I gave you your master's house and your master's wives into your keeping, and gave you the house of Israel and Judah. And if *that had been* too little, I also would have given you much more!'" Get that! God said, "If after all the blessings I've already showered you with wasn't enough, I would have given you MUCH MORE!" That's God's goodness giving David things that he didn't deserve!

Then here comes God's mercy toward David; in verse 13b, it says, "And Nathan said to David, 'The LORD also has put away your sin; you shall not die.'" That's God's mercy—keeping the punishment that he did deserve away from him!

It's no wonder that King David said in Psalm 23, "SURELY, goodness and mercy shall follow me all the days of my life!" Surely! As in being a done deal. Imagine that! As we go about in our daily lives, God's goodness *and* mercy are following right behind us! God is showing His goodness by giving us what we don't deserve and extending His mercy to us by keeping off us what we do deserve.

As a believer in Christ, it's not either/or; it's *both*!

Notes

He Restores My Soul!

He restores my soul.

—Psalm 23:3

"He restores my soul." What a beautiful promise from the Lord! Think about that for a moment; God restores your soul!

Your soul is made up of your mind, your will, and your emotions. I had recently gotten some bad news about a company that I was affiliated with, going out of business. My heart and mind was heavy during the slow, sluggish holiday sales season. I was concerned, not only about the company that I was doing business with, but also for the many other companies and jobs that were having such a hard time hanging on during these tough economic times. And then my heart and mind became very heavy when the announcement came that the doors were being shut.

What's a person to do when unfortunate news comes their way? Go directly to the Word of God! Don't pass "Go"; don't stop and collect two hundred bucks—go *straight to the Word of God!* King Solomon said in Ecclesiastes 1:9, "There is NOTHING new under the sun." Meaning, whatever you're going through, someone has gone through it before and came out victorious!

When I went to the Word of God, the Holy Spirit kept telling me, "He restores my soul." When I turned to the Twenty-third Psalm, I just couldn't get past those four little words—"He restores my soul."

Let me tell you what's packed into those four little words. It's like an overstuffed suitcase. The suitcase may look small on the outside, but when you open it up—WATCH OUT! Tons of things are going to come falling out of it!

He—the Lord!

Restores—brings back whatever has been lost or stolen, makes new again!

My—this is personal!

Soul—my mind, my will and my emotions.

God restores your mind, He straightens out your will to get going again, and He helps you to keep your emotions in check.

The Scripture goes on to say that He'll also lead you in the path of righteousness for His name's sake. His name is the Word, and He'll restore your soul for His name's sake because He's given you His Word on it!

For God's own sake, He'll restore your soul and get you going in the right direction again!

Notes

He Sends His Word to Heal Our Diseases!

Then they cried out to the LORD in their trouble, and He saved them out of their distresses. 20 He sent His word and healed them, and delivered them from their destructions.

—Psalm 107:19-20 (New King James Version)

Have you ever had a disease—or shall I say a dis-ease? Maybe not a physical ailment, but a spiritual, emotional, mental, or financial dis-ease, where you're so uncomfortable because of the status of your job or maybe you're still interceding for a loved one or still waiting for a doctor's report? If so, then *you need a Word from God!* Nothing else will do. In Matthew 8, the centurion soldier told Jesus, "Just speak A word and my servant will be healed."

God is *always* speaking, can you hear Him? As a matter of fact, as a child of God, His Word will track you down to make sure that you're comforted (or at ease) about your situation.

I remember being "uneasy" about the slow economy and feeling as though it was having a major impact on my business. The Lord sent His Word to me several times to say, "I'm going to bless you!" Those words first came to me from my mother who said the Lord told her to give me a message after spending time with Him in her private time. Next, the same message came to me from a devotional blog writer. God confirmed His Word again when I got into my car and turned on the radio. At first, I was inclined to change the channel, but then the words started tugging at my spirit, saying, "God is talking to you!" As I sat there listening to the song, the Lord ministered to me and gave me an assurance in my spirit that He heard my prayers.

God has no problem with confirming His Word to us either. He'd rather us know for sure that it's Him speaking than for us to assume it's Him when it may not be.

A few days later, I ran into my local grocery store and walked out with a Word from God! A *total stranger* was standing in line in front of me. She turned to me and said, "You have a ministry, don't you?" She went on to say, "The Lord is going to bless your ministry mightily, He's going to bless many people through it. I can see it in you."

Hallelujah! How's that for God's Word tracking you down?!

The Lord is never short on words. As a matter of fact, He's the Word who lives forever! He's *always* speaking and comforting His people. Are you listening?

Notes

In God's Presence!

In Your presence is fullness of joy; At Your right hand are pleasures forevermore.

—Psalm 16:11b

In the Old Testament of the Bible, only the high priest could go into God's presence, which was called the holies of holies. Now, because of Christ, all believers can go there.

Dr. Juanita Bynum calls it "the overflow." In her song of the same title, she says, it's *that* place where God pours His oil and where He shows His all! King David also referred to it as that "secret place." Why is it a secret? Because not everyone can enter into God's presence. It's a place of peace, joy, comfort, and safety. And it's where God wants us to dwell—not just to visit from time to time, but to *dwell*.

How do you get into God's presence, you may ask? By worshipping the Lord. Jesus told the Samaritan woman that the true worshippers would worship God in spirit and in truth. You don't have to wait until a certain day or time or get to a certain place; worship can take place at anytime and at any location. To get in God's presence, you have to be intimate with Him, and this can only be done through a personal relationship with Christ. When you worship God, you're testifying to *Him* about how good He is!

However, the presence of God should never be taken lightly—it's a holy place. In the book of Revelations, the Bible tells us that the four seraphim hover around the throne of God, and they do *not* rest, day or night—night or day—from saying, "Holy, holy, holy is the Lord." It's a place where the twenty-four elders cast down their golden crowns and fall at God's feet to worship Him.

In Luke 1, Zacharias had a hard time believing that he and his wife, Elizabeth, were going to conceive John the Baptist in their old age; the angel who delivered the message was like, "What?! I am Gabriel—and I stand in the presence of God—and I only speak what He tells me to say." What gave Gabriel such confidence and authority was the fact that he's privileged to be stationed in the very presence of God!

You could be on a crowded bus or train during rush hour and be sitting in your seat, worshipping God (no one hears anything); but while they're uptight, reading the newspaper, angry about having to go into the office, upset that someone got to the seat before they did, you can be in the very presence of God in your spirit!

You could be experiencing "hell on earth," but if you can just get into God's presence, it's a place where the enemy can't stand being around when the Lord is being worshipped in spirit and in truth.

In the very presence of God Himself—what a place to be!

Notes

Is There Anything Too Hard for God?

Behold, I am the LORD, the God of all flesh. Is there anything too hard for Me?

—Jeremiah 32:27

In reading the thirty-second chapter of Jeremiah, he does what the Lord tells him to do: he buys some land with cash and has the purchase witnessed by others (a legal transaction). Only to have the land that he purchased handed over to the Babylonians, who attacked the city and burned everything down to the ground. Jeremiah then prays to God for understanding as to why, in his obedience, was he witnessing such devastation.

In verse 27, the Lord answers him and says, "I AM THE LORD, the God of all flesh. IS THERE ANYTHING TOO HARD FOR ME?" While I am having this city destroyed because of the evil and wickedness that have taken place here, I'm going to *restore it*!

In verses 37 through 41, God says, "Not only will I gather my people and bring them back to this land, and not only will I make an everlasting covenant with them, and not only will I never stop doing GOOD to them, but I'm going to REJOICE IN DOING GOOD FOR THEM!" Think about that for a minute; not only will God never stop doing good for you, but it *pleases* Him, He rejoices over doing good for you!

In verses 42 through 44, God goes on to say that although this land is now a desolate waste, without people or animals, fields will be bought for money; deeds signed, sealed, and witnessed; and prosperity and fortunes will be restored. I don't know about you, but that sounds like an economical situation turning around to me!

Have you ever sat down and scratched your head or cried your tears over doing what you believe the Lord told you to do, but it only looks like everything is going wrong? I know that I have. The Lord asked Jeremiah whether there was anything too hard for Him. Despite Jeremiah's obedience, there were some things that God needed to destroy so that He could build something new and better on this same piece of land. And while it looks hopeless, keep in mind that *He is the Lord*!

Instead of telling God how big your problems are, you need to tell your problems how *big* your God is!

Maybe you can't turn your situation around yourself, *but* is there anything too hard for God?

Notes

It's All Working Together for Your Good!

And we know that all things work together for good to those who love God, to those who are the called according to His purpose.

—Romans 8: 28

Romans 8 is such a refreshing chapter in the Bible! Whenever you're in doubt about what you mean to the Lord, go straight to Romans 8 and read the entire chapter!

I had a book signing this past weekend, and a woman who I could clearly tell was walking with the Lord came to my table; she was all smiles, and you could see the joy of the Lord on her. However, when she read the titles (and subtitles) to my books, of which one is *Understanding Your Importance to the Lord*, it brought her to tears. And she said to me, "I have *got* to have that book! This is just what I need!" As I was signing it for her, the Lord told me to give her an encouraging word before she left, and she shared with me that she had a flight back home to the West Coast that same night, and that she was going to read the book on the airplane, and then she said, "Because I've been going through some stuff!"

Stuff! We all go through some things; and if we can just tell the truth about it, we all have periods in our lives when it seems as though everything is going wrong, and we wonder, "Where's God? Doesn't He see what I'm going through? Doesn't He still care about me?"

I know because I've been there!

Whenever life seems to be winning over you, and you're wondering if you'll make it through your situation, run directly to Romans 8! And here's why.

The chapter starts off by saying, "There is now no condemnation for those who are in Christ Jesus!" We can actually stop right there and get our praise on! But this chapter says so much more. It also tells us that we're going to go through some things or, as the sister put it, "stuff." Verse 18 says, "For I consider that the sufferings of this present time are not worthy *to be compared* with the glory which shall be revealed in us."

My sister is a certified gemologist. And she tells me of the "refining" or, shall we say, the "revealing" process that gold and diamonds have to go through before they become the objects of so many people's desires. Gold has to go through the fire several times, and diamonds have to be dug up from the earth and cut! Verse 18 tells us that the fire that we go through, the digging up, and the cutting processes are to reveal the glory that's in us!

But wait! There's so much more (as the commercial says)!

Verse 29 says that not only did God foreknow you, but

> He also predestined you to be conformed to the image of His Son, and not only are you Predestined,
> but you're also Called!
> And not only are you Foreknown by God, Predestined by God, and Called by God, but He's also Justified you!
> And not only are you Justified by God, but you're also Glorified by Him!

And if that weren't enough!

Verse 31 says if God is with you, then *who* can be against you?

Verse 32 says that God will freely give you all things!

Verse 33 says that you're God's elect!

Verse 34 says that Jesus is sitting at the right hand of God, *praying for you*!

Verse 35 says, *what on earth can separate you from the love of Christ*?!

Shall tribulation?

Shall distress?

Shall persecution?

Or famine?

Or nakedness?

Or peril?

Or sword?

These all sound like problems or "stuff" to me!

And it doesn't stop there! Verse 37 tells us that yet *in* all these things, you are *more than a conqueror* through Him who loves you!

And if that weren't enough! Paul goes on to say in verses 38 and 39 that he's *persuaded* that neither

> death,
> nor life,
> nor angels,
> nor principalities,
> nor powers,
> nor things present,
> nor things to come,
> nor height,
> nor depth,
> nor *anything created* shall be able to separate you from the love of
> God, which is in Christ Jesus our Lord!

Everything is working together for your own good. Uncut diamonds look like worthless rocks! They have to go through the "revealing" process. If you've ever questioned if God still cares about you, or if He still loves you, go *straight* to Romans 8!

Notes

.

Move Forward!

And the LORD said to Moses, "Why do you cry to Me? Tell the children of Israel to go forward."

—Exodus 14:15

I'm sure we've all seen the movie *The Ten Commandments*, and especially the Cecil B. DeMille version, starring the actor Charlton Heston. What's probably the most moving and awesome scene is when God opens the Red Sea so that the children of Israel can walk on dry ground and escape the pharaoh and his army and to continue on to reach the Promised Land.

Now, imagine here is Moses and the millions of the children of Israel at the banks of the Red Sea. *The Red Sea!* This is no small body of water. It's not a brook, a lake, or a stream, but a *huge* body of water, making it to look *impossible* to get to the other side of it. So you have the Red Sea on one side and pharaoh and his army who are in *hot* pursuit of you on the other side. And here comes the complaints from the children of Israel who are in the middle! In Exodus 14:11-12, "Then they said to Moses, 'Because *there were* no graves in Egypt, have you taken us away to die in the wilderness? Why have you so dealt with us, to bring us up out of Egypt? 12 *Is* this not the word that we told you in Egypt, saying, "Let us alone that we may serve the Egyptians?" For *it would have been* better for us to serve the Egyptians than that we should die in the wilderness.'"

Now, it would seem to me that that would be a fine time to start crying out to God, as Moses did, but notice God's response! In the fifteenth verse, God answered Moses and said, "Why do you cry to Me? Tell the children of Israel to go forward." I could imagine God was saying, "Yes, you're at the Red Sea, pharaoh is coming with his axmen, and the doubt and pressure from the children of Israel is mounting. While it may look impossible to get out of this situation alive, I promised to take you to the Promised Land, and this isn't it! While everything looks *totally impossible*, you're going to have to move *forward* on My Word that I've spoken to get to where I'm taking you!"

Wherever you are in life, what has God promised you? If you haven't reached your Promised Land yet, if you're not where God said that He was taking you—no matter what it looks like—keep moving *forward* on His Word!

As the late James Cleveland once said, "I don't believe He brought me this far just to leave me."

Notes

Perfected, Established, Strengthened, and Settled!

Resist him, steadfast in the faith, knowing that the same sufferings are experienced by your brotherhood in the world. 10 But may the God of all grace, who called us to His eternal glory by Christ Jesus, after you have suffered a while, perfect, establish, strengthen, and settle you. 11 To Him be the glory and the dominion forever and ever. Amen.

—1 Peter 5:9-11

Perfected, established, strengthened, and settled! Ahhhh, sounds like music to my ears. How do I get these? What? *After* I've suffered for a while!?

That's right! After we've suffered for a while, we have the great promise that the God of all grace will perfect us (make us mature in the things of God), establish, strengthen, and settle us. Who doesn't want this promise in these tough and rocky times? Everyone does, but very few want to suffer.

Suffering and troubles aren't bad; they're actually for our own good! Remember, *everything* is working together for your own good! (Rom. 8:28) It's lifting these heavy weights in life that cause us to build muscle, steadfastness, character, faith, and integrity! What athletic champion do you know who doesn't lift weights to build muscle so they can compete, and not only compete, but win the challenge?! What type of shape do you think Tiger Woods, Venus Williams, and others would have if they didn't build their muscles by lifting heavy weights? Would they be the champions that they are if they only did what's comfortable for them, like lifting two-pound dumbbells? Not at all!

In the movie *Slumdog Millionaire*, the main character became a millionaire by going on the game show, *Who Wants to Be a Millionaire*. But wait a minute. He didn't shed his life of extreme poverty just by going on the show. He had some very challenging trivia questions to answer. You've seen the show! He had no formal education, but was able to answer the questions based on all the trouble and pain he had experienced throughout his lifetime!

It was his sleeping in train cars, seeing his mother murdered as a child, being an orphan on the run, and practically being raised by his older brother (who was a child himself and later turned to a life of crime) that he was able to go through each level of success on the game show.

Peter also tells us to resist the devil and hold on to your faith! It's during the times of suffering that many of us start to question our faith. And as soon as the testing and sufferings come, here comes the devil! But Peter says to resist him and stick to your faith! He goes on to say that you're not in this alone, but know that others in the body of Christ (throughout the world) are also going through their own sufferings.

But it doesn't end there! Your suffering isn't going to last forever; it's only for a while. Meaning, it *will* come to an end! And who's going to perfect you, establish you, strengthen you, and settle you? The God of *all* grace! Peter doesn't just say that "God will perfect, establish, strengthen, and settle you," but he calls Him the God of *all* grace! Why is that important? Grace is specific. Grace is the favor (or gift) of God in various areas. For instance, when we read in the Word about spiritual gifts, it says in Romans 12:6, "Having then gifts DIFFERING ACCORDING TO THE GRACE that is given to use, let us use them." My spiritual gift is the gift of leadership (or in some translations, it's called the gift of administration). This is the grace (or gift) that God has given to me. I'm not as gifted in the other six spiritual gifts, but I've been given grace in leadership.

Kind of like Apple's slogan for their iPhone: "There's an app for that." They're telling you, whatever you want to do with your super-duper iPhone, there's a specific application that can do whatever you need done.

Well, whatever you're suffering through, there's a *grace* for that! If your area of suffering is depression, there's a *grace* for that! If it's fear that's bothering you, there's a *grace* for that! If it's lust, there's a *grace* for that! You name it, and there's a *grace* for it. Whatever you're suffering through, God will give you the favor to come out of it because He's the God of *all grace*! And after your "suffering for a while" is up, you will have built your spiritual muscles while you were going through it, and you'll find that He has kept His Word!

The world says, "Whatever doesn't kill you makes you stronger." The Word of God says that after you've suffered for a while, you will be perfected, you will be established, you will be strengthened, and you will be settled.

Glory to God!

Notes

Prayer Changes Things!

If My people who are called by My name will humble themselves, and pray and seek My face, and turn from their wicked ways, then I will hear from heaven, and will forgive their sin and heal their land.

—2 Chronicles 7:14

The ability and privilege to *personally communicate* with the God of the universe—that's what prayer is! A time when you can pour your thoughts, concerns, pains, and thanksgiving out to the Lord. And it's *prayer* that can change any situation.

In the Bible, we hear of people putting others out of the room and shutting the door so that they could pray. They also went up on rooftops, and Jesus went to the garden of Gethsemane—just to be alone with the Lord. In Matthew 6:6, Jesus said, "when you pray, go into your room and shut the door." This is *your* time with the Master! And He went on to say that the Father who sees you praying in your secret place will reward you openly! Yes, He's the God who sees, hears, speaks, and *lives!*

In 1 Kings 18, the prophet Elijah challenged the children of Israel by saying, "How long will you falter between two opinions? If the Lord is God, then follow Him. If Baal is god, then follow him." He then challenged the 450 prophets of Baal and said, "All of you, call upon your god, and I'll call upon the Lord, and the God who answers by fire, He is God."

So all 450 prophets of Baal called upon their god from morning until noon and received *no answer*. Elijah began to mock them around noon by saying, "Cry louder, maybe your god is sleeping and needs to be awakened, or maybe he's gone on a trip." So they continued to pray and even cut themselves until the blood poured out of them until *evening*. And the Bible says in 1 Kings 18:29, "But there was no voice; no one answered, no one paid attention."

Then here comes the lone prophet of the living God, Elijah, who commanded the people to flood the altar with water, *four* times over! Listen at Elijah's prayer in verse 36-37, "LORD God of Abraham, Isaac, and Israel, let it be known this day that You are God in Israel and I am Your servant, and that I have done all these things at Your word. 37 Hear me, O LORD, hear me, that this people may know that You are the LORD God, and that You have turned their hearts back to You again."

The Bible goes on to say that the fire of the Lord fell, consumed everything on the altar, and licked up every drop of water! And then all Israel fell down to worship the true and living God, the one who hears the prayers of His people!

It was *prayer* that caused God to add fifteen years to King Hezekiah's life! (2 Kings 20:1-6)

It was *prayer* that caused a barren Elizabeth to conceive John the Baptist in her old age (Luke 1:13).

It was Elijah's *prayer* that caused the heavens not to give rain for three and a half years (James 5:17).

Elijah *prayed* again, and the rain began to fall (James 5:18).

It was *prayer* that raised Dorcas from the dead (Acts 9:36-41).

As the old hymn says, "Oh, what peace we often forfeit / Oh, what needless pains we bear." Why? "All because we do *not* carry *everything to God in prayer!*"

Notes

Rejoice in Being Passed Over!

Then Moses called for all the elders of Israel and said to them, "Pick out and take lambs for yourselves according to your families, and kill the Passover lamb. 22 And you shall take a bunch of hyssop, dip it in the blood that is in the basin, and strike the lintel and the two doorposts with the blood that is in the basin. And none of you shall go out of the door of his house until morning. 23 For the LORD will pass through to strike the Egyptians; and when He sees the blood on the lintel and on the two doorposts, the LORD will pass over the door and not allow the destroyer to come into your houses to strike you."

—Exodus 12:21-23

Have you ever been passed over for something? Maybe a new job, a mate, or something that you thought you should have, but you didn't get?

In the book of Exodus, the children of Israel are finally about to be freed from their bondage. The Lord smote Egypt with ten plagues—*ten*—to show His many wondrous works in Egypt (Exod. 11:9). In the tenth and final plague, the Lord said in Exodus 12:4-7 that around midnight, He was going to go out into the midst of Egypt, and all the firstborn in the land was going to die. From the firstborn of Pharaoh to the firstborn of his servants and even the firstborn of the animals. Yes, not even the animals were excluded! Later on in the twelfth chapter, Moses gives instructions to the children of Israel and what they were to do to avoid this time of destruction.

In verse 21, Moses told the elders of Israel to pick out a lamb for their families and kill the Passover lamb, put its blood on the doorpost and lintel of their homes. He then said, "WHEN THE LORD SEES THE BLOOD—HE'S GOING TO PASS BY YOU AND NOT ALLOW THE DESTROYER TO COME INTO YOUR HOUSES TO STRIKE YOU."

Let me break that down for you a little bit and put it in modern-day terminology—the Bible says that destruction is coming! But when God sees the blood of the Passover Lamb (Jesus Christ) on the doorpost of your heart, He will *not* allow destruction to come in and destroy you.

Allow me to show you something; in Exodus 12, this is the first time that we're hearing about a "Passover lamb." In verse 21 of the same chapter, Moses tells the elders of Israel to take a lamb for your families and kill the Passover lamb. If you go back to verse 5, it describes what the Passover lamb is. It says that the Passover lamb needs to be without blemish (spotless), a male and the firstborn. Then later on in verse 27, Moses explains what's meant by "Passover." He said, "You'll tell your children that it's called the Passover sacrifice because when God saw THE BLOOD OF THE SPOTLESS LAMB, it was then that the destroyer passed over our houses when He came through to wipe out Egypt!"

1 Corinthians 5:7b says, "For indeed, Christ, our Passover, was sacrificed for us."

Maybe you're feeling depressed because you were passed over for a new job. It could be that God sees the future of that company and you don't, and within months, that job (and company) might fold, and it would be better for you to stay where you are! A friend of mine once told me that she was in love with a particular guy many years ago, and they never married. He "passed her over," only to find out that he not only killed his first wife, but also his second wife too! God had her passed over to spare her life!

King David said it this way in Psalm 90:7-8, "A thousand may fall at your side, and ten thousand at your right hand; *But* it shall not come near you. 8 Only with your eyes shall you look, and see the reward of the wicked."

Rejoice in God's perfect Passover Lamb!

Notes

Remember the Lord!

Moreover David said, "The LORD, who delivered me from the paw of the lion and from the paw of the bear, He will deliver me from the hand of this Philistine."

—1 Samuel 17:37

What are you stressing over today? A new challenge that has presented itself? A recent doctor's report? The current state of the economy or job market?

Sometimes, we need to take our eyes off the new, recent, or current, and *remember* what God has done for us in the past! Throughout the forty years that the children of Israel wondered through the wilderness, Moses constantly told them to remember how God freed them from the hand of pharaoh and the bondage of Egypt. He constantly reminded them of how God had already worked wonders for them to try and convince them to trust that God would continue to be with them.

In 1 Samuel 17, King Saul and the army of Israel are scared to death! They're battling against the Philistines, who send out their "champion," Goliath the giant. The Bible calls him a champion in verses 4 and 23, and it goes on to describe how huge he is in stature and how heavy his armor is. Verse 24 says, "And all the men of Israel, when they saw the man, fled from him and were dreadfully afraid." Grown men, dreadfully afraid!

Now, here comes David, Jesse's youngest of eight sons, and the smallest. David tells King Saul, in verse 32, that no one needs to be afraid of

Goliath because he's going to go out and fight him and kill him! King Saul says, "How are you going to do that when you're just a youth and this champion-giant has been fighting since he was a youth?" Then David starts to remember some things!

In verses 34-36, David says to Saul, "Your servant used to keep his father's sheep, and when a lion or a bear came and took a lamb out of the flock, 35 I went out after it and struck it and delivered the lamb from its mouth, and when it arose against me, I caught it by its beard and struck and killed it. 36 Your servant has killed both lion and bear; and this uncircumcised Philistine will be like one of them, seeing he has defied the armies of the living God."

These victories that David is talking about are past tense! Verse 37 says, "MOREVER David said, 'The LORD, who delivered me from the paw of the lion and from the paw of the bear, He will deliver me from the hand of this Philistine.'" David was so confident in God's track record that he said since He delivered me several times in the past, He WILL deliver me again!"

Oh, what confidence in God's power! Sometimes we don't need to ask God for anything new, just praise Him for what He's done in the past! Malachi 3:6 says, "For I am the Lord, I do NOT change." Hebrews 13:8 says, "Jesus Christ is the same yesterday and today and forever."

We need to remember if He provided for our parents, grandparents, or great grandparents during the Depression era, then He'll also provide for us during a recession. If He healed us of a headache last week, then He'll also heal us from high blood pressure this week! If He blessed us before, surely He'll do it again!

He is the Lord, and He does *not* change! Remember your past blessings and praise Him that He'll work everything out again!

Notes

Say Something!

Also He said to me, "Prophesy to the breath, prophesy, son of man, and say to the breath, 'Thus says the Lord GOD: "Come from the four winds, O breath, and breathe on these slain, that they may live."""

—Ezekiel 37: 9

In Ezekiel 37, we read the story of the dry bones. In the first fourteen verses, God turns a hopeless, dead situation around. He places Ezekiel in the *midst* of a valley *full* of dead dry bones and then tells Ezekiel to prophesy *three* times to the dry bones until the situation has life in it.

Are you right in the middle of a dry and lifeless situation? Where you look all around you and you only see dried-up hope, brokenness, and the impossible? God told Ezekiel, "*You* prophesy to this situation and *speak*, what thus says the Lord!"

The first time Ezekiel was told to prophesy was in verses 4-6, where God told him to tell this dried-up situation to "hear the Word of the Lord." He went on to say that God is going to breathe life into these bones, fill them with flesh, cover them with skin, and they shall live. Verse 7 says, "And then there was a RATTLING!" Where things start to look like they're turning around. But wait a minute, there was no breath in these bodies that God had put back together. Then in verse 9, God said to Ezekiel, "YOU prophesy again and command the winds to come from the four corners of the earth and breathe into this dead situation; that it may live."

So now Ezekiel has a great army of living and breathing people, but they have no hope. Then God says again, "Ezekiel, *you* tell them, 'I will open up their graves and bring them forth. I will put My Spirit in them and bring them to their own land and they *shall live!*'"

Speaking over your situation isn't a one-hit wonder. As we saw in Ezekiel 37, God told him to prophesy *three* times until the situation was what God intended it to be. But each time He said, "Ezekiel, *you* say something." It doesn't matter how bleak your situation may seem, whether it's healthwise, financial, mental, emotional, for a loved one, whatever—*speak* to your situation! Tell it constantly, "What thus says the Lord!" You may have to speak to it daily, but don't stop speaking God's Word over your matter until it's what God has promised you it would be.

Say something!

Notes

Sing Unto the Lord!

But at midnight Paul and Silas were praying and singing hymns to God, and the prisoners were listening to them. 26 Suddenly there was a great earthquake, so that the foundations of the prison were shaken; and immediately all the doors were opened and everyone's chains were loosed.

—Acts 16:25-26

Sing a song! Have you ever had a favorite song, or one that you've recently been singing in church that you can't seem to let go of? Some of us may be singing songs that we should let go of—songs of defeat, songs of doing things outside of the will of God, and songs that just talk about a bunch of drama!

Throughout the Psalms, David admonishes us to sing to the Lord!

In Psalm 33:3, he tells us to "sing to Him a new song."

In Psalm 68:4, he says, "Sing to God, sing praises to His name."

In Psalm 98:1, David says, "Oh, sing to the Lord a new song! For He has done marvelous things; His right hand and His holy arm have gained Him the victory."

In Psalm 105:2, he said, "Sing to Him, sing psalms to Him; talk of all of His wondrous works!"

In Psalm 149:3, he goes on to say, "Let them praise His name with the dance, let them sing praises to Him with the timbrel and harp."

Singing to God is written in the Bible over 150 times. Why singing? Singing comes from the heart. Ephesians 5:19 tells us, "Speaking to one another in psalms and hymns and spiritual songs, singing and making melody in your heart to the Lord."

While singing indicates joy, it doesn't necessarily come out of joyful situations. But something happens when you sing unto the Lord!

In 2 Chronicles, Judah is going to battle against Ammon, Moab, and Mount Seir—they are clearly outnumbered—but what do they do? They put the praise and worship team on the frontline of the battle! In verse 21, they sing a simple song to God, which says, "Praise the Lord, for His mercy endures forever." Then something happens in verse 22! The Bible tells us, "Now when they began to sing and to praise, the LORD set ambushes against the people of Ammon, Moab, and Mount Seir, who had come against Judah; and they were defeated."

When was the enemy defeated? When the people of God began to sing—not when they finished, but when they began!

Paul and Silas found themselves wrongly accused, beaten, and thrown in the inner part of the jail—not the outer part, but the inner part. In our modern-day vocabulary, that would be something like solitary confinement. Why were they there? Because they were doing the will of God and had cast demons out of a fortune-teller and her masters became upset for fear that they'd lose the profits they were making from her and had them imprisoned.

When Paul and Silas remembered in their hearts that while they may be imprisoned, the Lord was still on their side—they began singing and praising God. Not only did it bring freedom and victory to them, but also freedom to those around them! Because their singing and praising caused an earthquake, which caused all the prison doors to be opened and *everyone's* chains to fall off.

In 1873, Horatio Spafford penned the hymn "It Is Well With My Soul." Mr. Spafford's story is similar to Job's. In 1871, his only son died, and then there was the great Chicago Fire that year that ruined him financially. In 1873, he had planned to travel to Europe with his family but was delayed on business. The ship that was carrying his wife and four daughters collided with another ship and sank. His wife then sent him a telegram, which simply read, "Saved alone." When Mr. Spafford traveled to be with his grieving wife, while passing near the place where his daughters died, he was inspired to pen the words that say, "When peace like a river, attendeth my way, / When sorrows like sea billows roll; / Whatever my lot, Thou hast taught me to say, / It is well, it is well, with my soul."

No matter what you're going through, sometimes you just need to sing a song! Are you in a battle? Have you been beaten and falsely accused? Have you lost your family and/or finances?

Sing unto the Lord!

Notes

That Is His Name!

I am the LORD, that is My name.

—Isaiah 42:8a

What's in a name? In Genesis 2:19, when God gave Adam dominion over the Garden of Eden, He told Adam to name all the animals "and whatever you call them that's what they'll be!" When you think of a gorilla, the behaviors of a swan don't come to mind, do they? A name reveals the identity, nature, character, and essence of a person, place, or thing.

Several times in scriptures, God changed people's names when He changed their identity, character, and destiny. He changed Abram to Abraham to mean the father of many nations because that's who God said he'd be!

He changed Jacob's name, meaning trickster, which is exactly what he did to get his brother's birthright. His brother, Esau, said in Genesis 27:36 when he found out that his brother stole his birthright, "Is he not rightly named Jacob?" Meaning, he's acting just like his name! Jacob's name was later changed to Israel (Gen. 32:24-29). God visited Jacob, and he wouldn't let Him go until He blessed him! So Jacob wrestled with God all night; God then asked him what his name was, and he replied, "Jacob." The Lord then said, "Your name will not be called Jacob (trickster) but Israel (prince) because you have wrestled with God and man and have prevailed."

In the New Testament, Saul, the persecutor of the church, had an encounter with Jesus Himself and had to be called by a different name. Everyone knew Saul's identity as being one who tortured the followers of Christ; but when he was converted, he could no longer be called Saul but Paul, meaning filled with the Holy Spirit (Acts 13:9).

So what's in God's name?

When the Lord was sending Moses to deliver the children of Israel, Moses said to God, "'They're going to ask me Your name, what should I tell them?' And God said, 'I AM WHO I AM.' And He said, 'Thus you shall say to the children of Israel, "I AM" has sent me to you'" (Exod. 3:14).

Some may be thinking, "He is *what?*"

God's name is also Jehovah Tsidkenu, which means the Lord, our righteousness.

He's also Jehovah Mekaddsh, the God who Sanctifies.

He's Jehovah Shalom, the Lord of our peace.

He's also Jehovah Shammah, the God who's always there!

He's Jehovah Rophe, the God who heals.

He's also Jehovah Jireh, the God who provides.

He's Jehovah Nissi, the God who fights our battles and who is our banner!

He's Jehovah Rhoi, the Lord is our shepherd.

He's also El Shaddai, the God who's more than enough!

He's also El Elyon, the Most High God.

He's El Olam, the God of eternity.

He's El Berith, the God of the covenant (who keeps His Word!)

He's El Roi, the God who sees.

He's also El Hoseem, the God who creates.

He's whatever you need Him to be! His names tell us so!

Notes

Wait on the Lord!

But they that wait upon the LORD shall renew their strength; they shall mount up with wings as eagles; they shall run, and not be weary; and they shall walk, and not faint.

—Isaiah 40:31

Waiting on God: what a privilege!

In today's society of instantaneity, the thought of having to wait for just about anything is almost a foreign language or a lost art. Oh, but waiting on God has its privileges!

I've seen high-end department store staff members waiting (serving) celebrities in New York City as if they had nothing else to do, or no one else to serve, with the thoughts of receiving a nice commission once their wait was over. Or a waiter waiting with extreme patience on very affluent and high-powered people in Washington DC with the thought of receiving a very handsome tip once they were finished waiting. They would wait with a smile on their faces, while their strength was fading, and their feet and backs were killing them from standing for long periods and walking back and forth to the kitchen or stockroom to get their customers what they wanted.

And when they'd make it back to their customer, they had to wait some more because their patrons were saying to them, in essence, "I'm not done with you yet." All with the hopes of being "blessed" once they got their release.

There is no guarantee that waiting on mankind will result in any rewards, but God promises that His blessings are worth the *wait*! If you're waiting on Him to answer a prayer, then He's telling you that He's not done with you yet! You're probably wondering, "What do I do while I wait on the Lord?" You see what else He wants from you. What waiter doesn't check in to see what else he can serve his/her customers with—especially if he wants a good tip? God has never disappointed anyone who's waited on Him.

Job said in Job 14:14 that he'd *wait* on the Lord until his change would come! And we know that once the Lord "got through with him" he had *double the blessings for his trouble*!

David said in Psalm 27:14 to *wait* on the Lord and be of good courage, and He will strengthen your heart! He then said in Psalm 37:9 that those who *wait* on the Lord shall inherit the earth.

Lamentations 3:25 says that the Lord is good to those who *wait* for Him!

Isaiah said that those who *wait* upon the Lord, He shall renew their strength (strength while their waiting!) You shall mount up with wings as eagles (the most majestic bird of the air and the *only* bird that can fly *above the storms*!) And the benefits keep coming—you shall *run* and not grow weary, and you shall walk and not faint!

You're *guaranteed* strength while you're waiting, and blessings at the end of your wait!

Be of good courage. If you're waiting on God, count it a privilege, not everyone gets to wait on Him!

Notes

.

What to Do When You
Don't Know What to Do!

O our God, will You not judge them? For we have no power against this great multitude that is coming against us; nor do we know what to do, but our eyes are upon You.

—2 Chronicles 20:12

Let me just start by saying, "Get your praise on *now!*"

In reading 2 Chronicles 20, King Jehoshaphat and all Judah are in distress. They're fearful, and they're oppressed on every side! Coming against them to battle are the people of Moab, the people of Ammon, the people of Syria, and even some more folks! The Bible just calls them "others with them, besides the Ammonites."

King Jehoshaphat sets himself to seek the Lord, and he proclaimed a fast all throughout Judah. He then stands up in the assembly of Judah and Jerusalem in the house of the Lord and begins to *worship the Lord.* In verses 6 through 12, he just tells God how powerful He is and reminds God of how He won victories before for His people. He ends his worship by saying, "We have no power against this great multitude that is coming against us, nor do we know what to do, but our eyes are upon You."

Do you feel pressure and fear? Are things going wrong all around you? Do you feel as though you're under attack? Let's take a lesson from King Jehoshaphat and Judah. Before they presented their problems to the Lord, they *worshipped Him*! They told Him how powerful He is and said (and I paraphrased), "Only *You*, O God, can help us with these problems. And I'm going to see how You'll work this out on our behalf!"

God, who never leaves anyone hanging, sent His Word through Jahaziel and said in verse 15, "Listen, do NOT be afraid nor dismayed because of this great multitude, for the battle is NOT yours, BUT GOD'S!" In verse 17, He said, "You will NOT need to fight in this battle. Position yourselves, STAND STILL AND SEE THE SALVATION OF THE LORD, Who is with you!"

In verses 18 and 19, Jehoshaphat and all Judah and Jerusalem bowed before the Lord to *worship* Him, and the Levites stood up to *praise* Him.

But wait a minute! The battle is on *tomorrow*, and they're already getting their praise and worship on!

In verse 21, Jehoshaphat begins to appoint those who would *sing to the Lord* and those who would *praise* the beauty of His holiness before the army. Then it happens! In verse 22, it says, "Now WHEN they began to SING and to PRAISE, the Lord set ambushes against all of their enemies." Their enemies began to destroy one another, and the battle was *not* won by the sword, but by praising and worshipping God!

Whatever your battles are, put your eyes on the Lord, and then *get your praise and worship on* and watch Him work it out!

Notes

With Thanksgiving!

Be anxious for nothing, but in everything by prayer and supplication, with thanksgiving, let your requests be made known to God; 7 and the peace of God, which surpasses all understanding, will guard your hearts and minds through Christ Jesus.

—Philippians 4:6-7

I love the above scripture! Be anxious for nothing; in other words, don't worry about anything! Instead, *pray* about it! Notice that the writer of Philippians didn't just say, "But in everything by prayer and supplication let your requests be made known to God." Right in the middle of that statement he says, "With thanksgiving, let your requests be made known to God." With thanksgiving!

How often do we pray and just simply dump our laundry list of needs and wants on to God's altar? We pray like, "Lord, please bless me with a new job—I just can't take it there anymore. And bless me with a new car, my transmission died today. The car already had dents and scratches, and the heat is no longer working, so I just need a new car. Lord, we also need a new house—we've outgrown our current home. And Lord, please bless the children with good grades this semester. In Jesus's name. Amen."

The scripture says, "With thanksgiving, let your requests be made known to God." Instead, why don't we try praying, "Lord, I thank You for the job that I do have. I thank You for the income to feed and clothe my family! So many people are without income, but I give You thanks for what we do have. And Lord, thank You for a roof over our heads! I'm so grateful that we're not living outdoors. I give You praise that my children are still in their right minds and in the land of the living!"

The scripture goes on to say in verse 7, "And the peace of God, which surpasses all understanding, will guard your hearts and minds through Christ Jesus." And the *peace of God!* It's one thing not to worry about things and to be at peace—but to have the *peace of God!* The word "of" is a preposition, which is used to show possession or direction from. So this scripture is saying, God's peace! The same peace that God Himself has!

Let's put it all together. Philippians 4:6-7 is telling us not to worry about *anything*—but pray to God about *everything*—and give Him *thanks* for what He's already done, and make your requests known to Him. And once you've done that, the peace of God will come over you. The kind of peace that you can't even explain! And the things that you should be stressed out over won't cause you to have heart attacks, nervous breakdowns, and the like because God's peace is guarding over your heart and mind (*His* peace—*Your* heart and mind). And you have access to the same peace that God has because of your relationship with Him through Jesus Christ!

With thanksgiving!

Notes

Puzzles

Jazz!
Aleysha R. Proctor

```
r e t n e c y d e n n e k e h t o o m s g c
s r a p e m c i t b l v i n d y p d a k t i
s t b s m u o s a x o p h o n e h r e l c y
a a i l n t t n n c s r r h r l d a t y o h
c c t o u a d c a e j n u p c h y o m m o n
c h d u k c c l l i n g t o n a r b a b u o
i t r a c c s l t c p m u r t r a y t c u o
c n t c u h i a r n c h u c k l o c b o l i
s l a c c g r f l o c t r i s c f k a g o y
s o c t y a n i r l w i r m i m t a s o u j
i c f z r t r t s h c c s i l l c t c l l c
v n z z a u d z t b k y n s c o l h w t s l
a l z c r s m g r o o v y t u g c c o l a p
d l a r o t h c c o t t o n c l u b l s r c
s n j t p r b r n a n z t c y g d i f t m c
c c h m m c c a z t u b r i c r j r t s s n
l g r c c c h l s f a s c g u a l c r a t c
i d n a t t h d c s w l r m z z c h a h r a
m o i u n d t i i i c o s z a d u m p s o o
c n l s o c s c n r o h a n c l h c o p n d
c f p w c t a g o v h g c o i d a r r c g l
t c i n p s l l c g c n d s y r c c d c o c
```

band
bass
Blues Alley
Chris Botti
Chuck Loeb
contemporary
Count Basie
cymbals
Dizzy Gillespie
drums
Duke Ellington
electric guitar
Ella Fitzgerald
Fuge Groove
flute
groovy
Harlem
instrumentals
Jazz Age
jazz fest
keyboard
legends
Lena Horne
Lincoln Theatre
Louis Armstrong
microphone
Miles Davis
New Orleans
piano
radio
saxophone
smooth
swing
The Birchmere
The Cotton Club
The Kennedy Center
trumpet
U Street DC
vocals
Wolf Trap

Jazz-All Mixed Up

Rumsd
Opxsohnea
Oinlvi
Rpah
Tairgu
Rptuetm
Eykboard
Isenrg
Rconoutcd
Tohmso
Apt cedrsan
Ushcor Isgir
Gib nadb scmui
Emrhal
Odiar
Vsiflesta
Renctoc
Abc olcwalya
Inabgejso
Aer
Eenaj
Cdrriha lioelt
Awertl asbeely
Oarnmn owrnb
Islem ivdas
Eht eudk
Igrornmfep rtas
Ucsim
Hmorayn
Hytrhm

All That Jazz! The Crossword Puzzle
Aleysha R. Proctor

Across

3 Song made famous by the Dave Brubeck Band. (2 words)
5 Instrument played by Boney James.
6 _____ Vaughan
9 Lady Sings the Blues. (2 words)
12 Brothers: Branford and Wynton
14 Musical era from 1897 to 1918.
16 Contemporary jazz.
17 Grover _____, Jr.
18 "On Broadway". (2 words)

Down

1 Legends of Jazz radio show. (2 words)
2 _____ G.
4 Paul Hardcastle's group.
7 The Hi De Ho Man. (2 words)
8 _____ Gillespie.
10 There's a statue of him in the New Orleans airport. (2 words)
11 Birth of the Cool. (2 words)
13 The Duke.
15 Ella Fitzgerald was known for this type of singing.

Java!
Aleysha R. Proctor

```
a c v e f i l n b r p e c c a l c s
c k f n f a v h u u n s c o o p a a
b n l f e d a h c o m a c t o u o i
m v a u o z t e c v v p a n c k n b
c r s l e o e s s a t i m e d e i l
e a o l c f r e n c h p r e s s c e
a g n b f n c i r c r c w h a s c n
n u a o t o l b c l d e c a f l u d
t s c d i l a a e s r s a e f o p s
b t i i a t m m n b y p f m r w p c
d r r e l r a a h r a r f l a r a k
r r e d u r e s u o h e e f f o c b
m m m v a b c p r p o s m c a a i o
e f a c e r f m a e t s i f l s d c
n m r l f j f u a a v o s b t t p k
c r o t a l o c r e p n t r e l l e
j h m v c l c v b i s c o t t i o r
w l a t t e c o p e n m i c m c s u
```

americano
aroma
biscotti
bistro
black
blend
breve
cafe
cafe au lait
caffe nisto
cappuccino
caramel
coffee
coffee cup
coffeehouse
conversation
cookie
cream
decaf
demitasse
espresso
foam
french press
fresh brewed
full bodied
hazelnut
java
latte
macchiato
milk
mocha
open mic
percolator
saucer
scone
scoop
slow roast
steam
sugar
syrup
vanilla
whole beans

Java - All Mixed Up!
Aleysha R. Proctor

eecffo

feca

vereb

ucoehefsfoe

ostcanrivnoe

amaro

dnbel

iallnav

ocamh

nconmnia

tsmea

afmo

linspresk

ecmar

oncccipuap

hweol bneas

isatnp

rfmersa

liant eiramca

aaicrf

isaa

flul ddieob

soessper

caef ualita

camarnoei

tltae

okcioe

tcboitis

pcu fo oje

riedn

eecffomrake

tfrleis

snecso

Java! The Crossword Puzzle
Aleysha R. Proctor

Across

4 Cafe _____.
7 Nothing needed.
8 Highly concentrated.
10 _____ macchiato.
12 Device used to steep coffee. (2 words)
14 Coffee's negative health effect.
17 Use ice. (2 words)
18 Just add water and stir.
19 _____ syrups.
20 Just add water and brew. (2 words)

Down

1 Steamed milk.
2 All coffee is _____ before it's consumed.
3 Mix it all together.
5 Slang for coffee. (3 words)
6 Made of paper, plastic or metal.
9 Needs to be grinded.
11 Named after American soldiers in World War II.
13 Social gathering place.
15 Small bistro.
16 _____ latte.

Jesus!
Aleysha R. Proctor

```
a  g  s  s  m  e  v  l  j  i  s  h  w  o  i  r  e
r  e  g  a  h  e  y  i  n  a  p  w  l  s  y  i  a
y  r  h  m  v  h  l  o  r  e  v  o  s  s  a  p  s
n  o  i  t  a  v  l  a  s  g  r  c  h  r  i  s  t
o  v  i  s  g  i  i  o  s  d  i  o  d  s  t  k  e
h  t  c  i  r  o  j  u  a  u  l  n  h  t  i  p  r
a  h  t  r  a  m  d  n  a  y  r  a  m  n  s  l  o
i  e  g  h  u  m  s  t  t  l  d  e  g  a  u  l  i
s  o  y  c  n  c  u  r  h  u  h  o  j  h  r  t  v
s  n  e  m  e  s  i  w  j  e  f  a  l  e  a  y  a
e  l  e  a  s  n  a  f  l  k  s  e  d  a  z  r  s
m  y  m  l  i  i  o  h  i  i  s  o  o  l  a  n  m
a  w  r  t  r  n  t  n  i  x  r  i  n  i  l  m  a
l  a  y  i  o  e  g  p  c  e  i  e  t  n  f  n  s
i  y  a  i  b  s  a  l  a  m  b  o  f  g  o  d  t
s  e  l  p  i  c  s  i  d  b  m  a  n  g  e  r  e
y  g  t  r  a  a  h  n  o  b  i  s  e  s  t  a  r
```

baptism
Bethlehem
Christ
Christmas
crucifixion
disciples
Easter
God the Son
healing
Holy Trinity
Jerusalem
Joseph
King of Kings
Lamb of God
Lazarus
Lion of Judah
Lord
manger
Mary and Martha
Master
Messiah
Passover
risen
salvation
Savior
star
the only way
tomb
Virgin Mary
wise men

Jesus! The Word Search Puzzle
Aleysha R. Proctor

seusj

rgiivnmayr

nso fog do

cirenp fo acpee

lheera

lodob

rscso

wto evtiesh

disipclse

pitmabs

cmiogn ckba

ilostavna

amen

wrdo fo ogd

awtre not i wnei

enhaev

thehlbmee

lbnid amn

susei fo lbood

mlteep

kyenod

psosarev

amlb

staef

rdeib

irrgmaea

eirns

idrthyad

hastmsirc

yprear

Jesus - Who is He?!
Aleysha R. Proctor

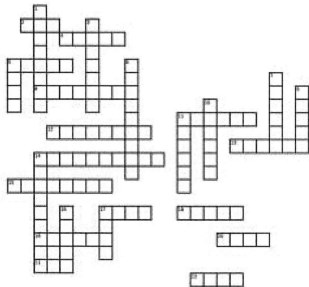

Across

2 The Only _____ to God.
4 The _____ that the builders rejected.
5 Hope of _____
8 And His name shall be called _____
11 High _____
12 _____ with the Father
13 The Head of the _____.
14 Marriage Supper _____
15 The Only _____ Son of God.
17 _____ of Lords
18 The Way, the _____ and the Life.
19 The Mighty One of _____.
20 _____ of Kings
21 Lamb of _____
22 _____ of God

Down

1 _____ Lamb
3 Bright and _____ Star
5 _____ Shepherd
6 Horn of _____
7 _____ of our souls
9 Lion of the Tribe of _____
10 _____ Water
11 _____ of Peace
14 _____ and the End
16 Light of the _____
17 _____ of the Valley

Answer Keys

Jazz!
Aleysha R. Proctor

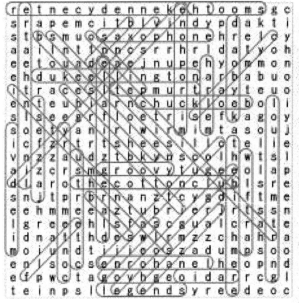

band
bass
Blues Alley
Chris Botti
Chuck Loeb
contemporary
Count Basie
cymbals
Dizzy Gillespie
drums
Duke Ellington
electric guitar
Ella Fitzgerald
Euge Groove
flute
groovy
Harlem
instrumentals
Jazz Age
jazz fest
keyboard
legends
Lena Horne
Lincoln Theatre
Louis Armstrong
microphone
Miles Davis
New Orleans
piano
radio
saxophone
smooth
swing
The Birchmere
The Cotton Club
The Kennedy Center
trumpet
U Street DC
vocals
Wolf Trap

Jazz – All Mixed Up!
Aleysha R. Proctor

rumsd	drums
opxsohnea	saxophone
oinlvi	violin
rpah	harp
tairgu	guitar
rptuetm	trumpet
eykboard	keyboard
isenrg	singer
rconoutcd	conductor
tohmso	smooth
apt cedrsan	tap dancers
ushcor lsgir	chorus girls
gib nadb scmui	big band music
emrhal	harlem
odiar	radio
vsiflesta	festivals
renctoc	concert
abc olcwalya	calloway
lnabgejso	bojangles
aer	era
eenaj	najee
cdrriha lioelt	richard elliot
awertl asbeely	walter beasley
oarnmn owrnb	norman brown
islem ivdas	miles davis
eht eudk	the duke
igrornmfep rtas	performing arts
ucsim	music
hmorayn	harmony
hytrhm	rhythm

All That Jazz! The Crossword Puzzle
Aleysha R. Proctor

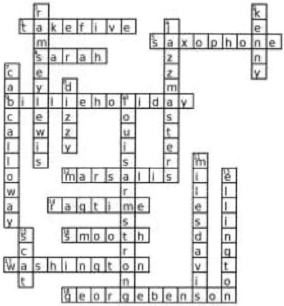

Across

3 Song made famous by the Dave Brubeck Band. (2 words)
5 Instrument played by Boney James.
6 _____ Vaughan
9 Lady Sings the Blues. (2 words)
12 Brothers: Branford and Wynton
14 Musical era from 1897 to 1918.
16 Contemporary jazz.
17 Grover _____, Jr.
18 "On Broadway". (2 words)

Down

1 Legends of Jazz radio show. (2 words)
2 _____ G.
4 Paul Hardcastle's group.
7 The Hi De Ho Man. (2 words)
8 _____ Gillespie.
10 There's a statue of him in the New Orleans airport. (2 words)
11 Birth of the Cool. (2 words)
13 The Duke.
15 Ella Fitzgerald was known for this type of singing.

Java!
Aleysha R. Proctor

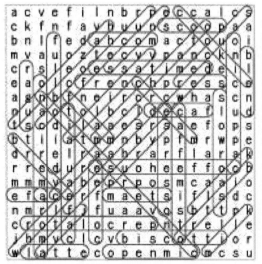

americano
aroma
biscotti
bistro
black
blend
breve
cafe
cafe au lait
caffe nisto
cappuccino
caramel
coffee
coffee cup
coffeehouse
conversation
cookie
cream
decaf
demitasse
espresso
foam
french press
fresh brewed
full bodied
hazelnut
java
latte
macchiato
milk
mocha
open mic
percolator
saucer
scone
scoop
slow roast
steam
sugar
syrup
vanilla
whole beans

Java - All Mixed Up!
Aleysha R. Proctor

eecffo	coffee
feca	cafe
vereb	breve
ucoehefsfoe	coffeehouse
ostcanrivnoe	conversation
amaro	aroma
dnbel	blend
iallnav	vanilla
ocamh	mocha
nconmnia	cinnamon
tsmea	steam
afmo	foam
linspresk	sprinkles
ecmar	cream
oncccipuap	cappuccino
hweol bneas	whole beans
lsatnp	plants
rfmersa	farmers
liant eiramca	latin america
aaicrf	africa
isaa	asia
flul ddieob	full bodied
soessper	espresso
caef ua llta	cafe au lait
camarnoel	americano
tltae	latte
okcioe	cookie
tcboitis	biscotti
pcu fo oje	cup of joe
rledn	diner
eecffo mrake	coffee maker
tfrleis	filters
snecso	scones

Java! The Crossword Puzzle
Aleysha R. Proctor

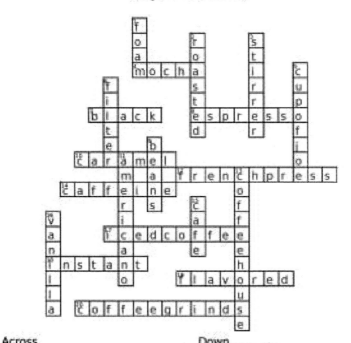

Across

4 Cafe _____.
7 Nothing needed.
8 Highly concentrated.
10 _____ macchiato.
12 Device used to steep coffee. (2 words)
14 Coffee's negative health effect.
17 Use ice. (2 words)
18 Just add water and stir.
19 _____ syrups.
20 Just add water and brew. (2 words)

Down

1 Steamed milk.
2 All coffee is _____ before it's consumed.
3 Mix it all together.
5 Slang for coffee. (3 words)
6 Made of paper, plastic or metal.
9 Needs to be grinded.
11 Named after American soldiers in World War II.
13 Social gathering place.
15 Small bistro.
16 _____ latte.

Jesus!
Aleysha R. Proctor

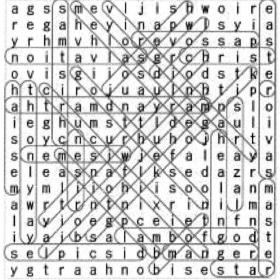

baptism
Bethlehem
Christ
Christmas
crucifixion
disciples
Easter
God the Son
healing
Holy Trinity
Jerusalem
Joseph
King of Kings
Lamb of God
Lazarus
Lion of Judah
Lord
manger
Mary and Martha
Master
Messiah
Passover
risen
salvation
Savior
star
the only way
tomb
Virgin Mary
wise men

Jesus! The Word Search Puzzle
Aleysha R. Proctor

seusj	jesus
rgiivnmayr	virgin mary
nso fo gdo	son of god
cirenp fo acpee	prince of peace
lheera	healer
lodob	blood
rscso	cross
wto evtiesh	two thieves
disipclse	disciples
pitmabs	baptism
cmiogn ckba	coming back
ilostavna	salvation
amen	name
wrdo fo ogd	word of god
atwre noti wnei	water into wine
enhaev	heaven
thehlbmee	bethlehem
lbnid amn	blind man
susei fo lbood	issue of blood
mlteep	temple
kyenod	donkey
psosarev	passover
amlb	lamb
staef	feast
rdeib	bride
irrgmaea	marriage
eirns	risen
idrth yad	third day
hastmsirc	christmas
yprear	prayer

Jesus - Who is He?!
Aleysha R. Proctor

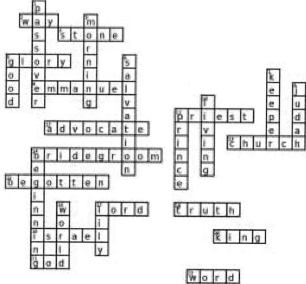

Across

2 The Only _____ to God.
4 The _____ that the builders rejected.
5 Hope of _____
8 And His name shall be called

11 High _____
12 _____ with the Father
13 The Head of the _____.
14 Marriage Supper
15 The Only _____ Son of God.
17 _____ of Lords
18 The Way, the _____ and the Life.
19 The Mighty One of _____.
20 _____ of Kings
21 Lamb of _____
22 _____ of God

Down

1 _____ Lamb
3 Bright and _____ Star
5 _____ Shepherd
6 Horn of _____
7 _____ of our souls
9 Lion of the Tribe of _____
10 _____ Water
11 _____ of Peace
14 _____ and the End
16 Light of the _____
17 _____ of the Valley